Shubnell's Profound Thoughts

Book 1

Great Thoughts from Great Minds
About Life, Time, and Ageing
for
Executives, Speakers, Writers, and just
about Everyone

Thomas F. Shubnell, Ph.D.

ISBN - 1448621984
EAN - 9781448621989

Cover and interior design by TFS

Autohagiography

If you enjoy this, you will also love, "Gracious Me . . . Is Nothing Sacred." A non-sectarian and hilarious look at all religions from the beginning of time. It truly proves that laughter is good for the soul.

Medical humor abounds in the best selling "Medical Humor" medical nonsense to tickle your funnybone. A great collection of medical funny stuff, including stories, jokes, and hilarious pictures and cartoons.

Another wacky book, "Men vs. Women, a Book of Lists" examines life from a different perspective and tells it all - the differences between the sexes are real and funny.

Speaking of wacky, why not read, "Number One book of Wacky Lists", a hilarious compendium of lists from the sublime to the absurd. Interesting facts and bits of wisdom, humor, and just plain common sense. Something for everyone to enjoy.

Even more fun can be found in "The Best of Terrible Tommy and Yucky Chucky," a collection of the best Terrible Tommy and Yucky Chucky jokes of all time.

More hilarious reading can be found in "Giggles, Gags, and Quips, Special Picks" a collection of the best jokes, pictures, billboards, stories, and cartoons.

Also collect all the "Greatest Jokes of the Century" series of books. 25 wildly funny and hilarious compendiums of the greatest jokes, tidbits, stories, and trivia that are sure to induce uncontrollable laughter. The best bathroom reading since Readers Digest.

Don't forget to collect the rest of the Profound Thoughts series.

All written by Thomas F. Shubnell and available at Amazon.com
Also ask for them at your favorite bookstore or as ebooks at shubsbooks.com

Tab e of Contents

Life

Enjoy life - This is not a rehearsal.

Life is like a bath - the longer you stay in it, the more wrinkled you get.

There are three stages of life - youth, middle age, and "You're looking well."

Life is like a bicycle, you don't fall off unless you stop pedaling.

Make the most of all that comes in life and the least of all that goes.

Life is what you make of it - kind of like Play-Doh.

What a world - everybody asks how you're feeling, then acts bored when you begin to tell them.

If God hadn't intended us to be happy, he wouldn't have made it so easy for us to smile.

You can live in this world only once, but if you live right, once is enough.

Life is not a problem to be solved, but a gift to be enjoyed.

Character is not what you are thought to be, but are.

Life

Those who convert dreams into reality have done the most to advance civilization.

Life doesn't require that we be the best, only that we try our best.

You can't experience life without feeling life.

Let us be of good cheer, remembering that the misfortunes hardest to bear are those which never come.

A pessimist takes life with a grain of sulk.

The school of life is a compulsory education that no one escapes.

People are not masters of the planet, only guests.

Count your life by smiles not tears.
Count you age by friends, not years.

There are two kinds of people who don't say much - those who are quiet and those who talk a lot.

In life most of the mountains we climb we built ourselves.

The smallest good deed is better than the greatest good intention.

You cannot live a perfect day without doing something for someone who will never be able to repay you.

Every person cannot be the best, but every person can be his or her best.

The first test of a truly great man is his humility.

Only you can be yourself. No one else is qualified for the job.

Those persons who are always dog-tired like to growl about it.

Patience is the virtue of life.

Some days you are the bug. Some days you are the windshield.

The naked truth is more appealing when it's pressed in a smile.

Looking at the bright side of things will improve, not damage, your insight.

All our dreams can come true, if we have the courage to pursue them.

The easiest thing to keep in your head is a cold.

Life is ten percent what happens to you and ninety percent how you react to it.

The state of your life is nothing more than a reflection of your state of mind.

The truth is, if one of us succeeds, we all do.

Nothing great in the world has been accomplished without passion.

I can keep a secret, but those I tell it to never can.

Life

It is better to look ahead and prepare than to look back and regret.

Your life lies before you like a path of driven snow, be careful how you tread it, because every step will show.

The smallest light is seen in the darkest night.

One of the heaviest pieces of baggage to carry through life is a chip on the shoulder.

The nice thing about being imperfect is the joy it brings to others.

Keep old memories and young hopes.

The only people who find what they are looking for in life are the fault finders.

Tough times never last, tough people do.

People get most tired when they are standing still.

When a man is wrapped up in himself, he makes a very small package.

Life is what we make it -
always has been,
always will be.

Those who know how to enjoy life are not poor.

Two of life's great challenges are keeping your weight down and your spirits up.

A moment's insight is sometimes worth a life's experience.

It is difficult to have rosy thoughts of the future when your mind is full of the blues of the past.

A life that touches the hearts of others goes on forever.

There are only two ways to live your life. One is as though nothing is a miracle. The other is as though everything is a miracle.

Good, better, best - never rest until good is better and better is best.

Life is a continuous process of getting used to the things we hadn't expected.

Success in life comes not from holding a good hand, but in playing a poor hand well.

People who sing their own praises are apt to be soloists.

Courage is important. Like a muscle, it's strengthened by use.

The best way to lighten life's load is by lifting a weight off someone else's back.

No man is a failure who is enjoying life.

In the game of life, it's easier to see the goalposts if you keep your chin up.

Life is tough after the kids leave home and you have no one to blame for things, but each other.

Life

Vitality! That's the pursuit of life, isn't it?

Hope sees the invisible,
feels the intangible,
and achieves the impossible.

Life is a great big canvas; you should throw all the paint on it
you can.

Life is a choice of values.

Shoot for the moon and even if you miss it, you will land
among the stars.

One cannot say he has lived unless he has helped another to do
so.

To overlook the little things in life is to miss the biggest part of
life itself.

Life can be understood by looking backward, but it must be
lived by looking forward.

Life is like a roll of toilet paper. The closer it gets to the end,
the faster it goes.

The less of routine, the more of life.

Don't just live and let live, live and help live.

What counts in life is what we do for others.

The hardest thing to learn in life is which bridge to cross and
which to burn.

It's choice, not chance, that determines your destiny.

If you want the rainbow, you have to put up with the rain.

Just as important as what happens to you in this life is how you take it.

Don't leave God out of your life.

Life may be like a game of cards;
we cannot help the hand that is dealt us,
but we can help the way we play it.

Courage, faith, modesty, and humor are the keys to life's doors.

Make yourself useful as well as ornamental.

Life is what happens to you when you're making other plans.

Need, by nature, is the same - no matter how or to whom it came.

Fit yourself into accord with the things in which it has been your lot to have been cast.

Life is a picture - paint it well.

Many talented persons drift aimlessly through life; a purpose will give true meaning for living.

Tame the savageness of man and make gentle the life of the world.

Life

No one can hinder you from saying or doing what is in accordance with nature.

Giving up on yourself is a crime, and it carries a life sentence.

Life is short,
art long,
opportunity fleeting,
experience treacherous,
judgment difficult.

Life is too important to be taken seriously.

Playing golf is different from life - in golf you try to get into a hole, in life you don't have to try.

Those whom we support hold us up in life.

If I end up disappointed with my life, it'll be because of what I have done, not failed to do.

One of the problems with living on the edge is that there is so little room for error.

There's only one thing more painful than learning from experience, and that is not learning from experience.

Do you ever feel like life is a car wash and you're going through it on a bicycle?

Things in life even out pretty well. Others people's troubles are not as bad as ours, but their children are a lot worse.

To know that even one life has breathed easier because you have lived is to have succeeded.

The only hell a person needs is to have his eyes opened to the person he might have been.

Life is not measured in hours, but in accomplishments.

People who cut themselves off from God are left with only frail human resources to live by.

One of life's great pleasures is coming up to your illegally parked car and not finding a ticket on it.

There are lights and shadows that make your life deep and strong.

It's a funny thing about life: If you refuse to accept anything but the best, you often get it.

Have faith in what you believe and don't give up on the future. Today's dream is the threshold of tomorrow's discovery.

More things grow in the garden than the gardener sows.

Self-esteem is feeling good about yourself, regardless of the facts.

The meaning of life is to make your own life meaningful.

The pleasure you get from life is equal to the attitude you put into it.

Look back on your life like a good day's work.

Life

Fill your life with experiences not excuses.

Every good thought you think is contributing its share to the ultimate result of your life.

Live life with intensity.

Life is like a ladder, every step we take is either up or down.

Life is a tragedy to those who feel,
but a comedy to those who think.

We make a living by what we get;
we make a life by what we give.

If life seems like it is all uphill, you must be reaching your peak.

Knowing how to make a living is important, but never as important as knowing how to live.

Next to knowing when to seize an opportunity, the most important thing in life is to know when to forgo an advantage.

To avoid criticism, do nothing, say nothing, be nothing.

One nice thing about living alone, all decisions are unanimous.

Being a survivor must mean more than just staying alive.

Change is not really an optional thing.

Accept that some days you are the pigeon, and some days you are the statue.

Words are plentiful, but deeds are precious.

We all take different paths in life, but no matter where we go, we take a little of each other everywhere.

Hot heads and cold hearts never solved anything.

Never drive faster than your angel can fly.

There are only two shoulders you can rely on, and they both belong to you.

One of the secrets of a happy life is continuous small treats.

Health is the greatest gift,
contentment the greatest wealth,
faithfulness the best relationship.

It's alright letting yourself go as long as you can let yourself back.

Life is too marvelous, too brimming with color for me to get tired.

Attitude is everything, that's what will determine the quality of your life.

Learn to listen; opportunity may be knocking at your door very softly.

There is more to life than increasing its speed.

Life

Having the right aim in life isn't enough if you run out of ammunition.

The trouble with life is you're halfway through it before you realize it's a do-it-yourself project.

The secret of life is not to do what you like, but to like what you do.

You have to take life as it happens, but you should try to make it happen the way you want to take it.

Loneliness doesn't tell you what you have lost; only that something is missing.

Learn the joy of giving, for when you only receive you miss much of life.

If you never have a dream, you will never have a dream come true.

If you want to leave footprints in the sands of time, don't drag your feet.

Contentment is contagious.

The most effective water power in the world is tears.

Life's heaviest burden is to have nothing to carry.

Life is no better if we worry;
life is no better if we hurry.

As long as we are changing, we are living.

The secret to enjoying life is to count your blessings - not your birthdays.

The Golden Rule has no inches or feet, yet it is the measure of every man.

The greatest wastes in life are untried ideas and unused talents.

Miracles, when aided and abetted by determined action, do happen.

More often than we realize, what we didn't achieve, we didn't want.

One of the toughest lessons in life is learning to expect the unexpected.

Man is in possession of his own life when he can control his thoughts, rule his passions, and govern his habits.

People who rush through life shouldn't be too surprised if they get to the end a little sooner than anticipated.

Never give people a chance to reach any conclusion about you, but the one you want.

Not one shred of evidence supports the notion that life is serious.

Fear of change causes some persons to be:
comfortable in their misery,
secure in their mediocrity, and
paralyzed in their prejudice.

Life

Don't worry about other people making a fool of you. That is strictly a do-it-yourself project.

It's not about where you're going. It's about what you leave behind.

Some people are born mediocre,
some people achieve mediocrity, and
some people have mediocrity thrust upon them.

People who walk in another's tracks leave no prints.

Opportunity may knock, but it will never open the door on its own.

If it weren't for underachievers, no one could be above average.

A great pleasure in life is doing what others say you can't.

Life should be deeper than it is long.

A #2 pencil and a dream can take you anywhere.

The art of life is knowing the right time to say things.

Life may not be the party we hoped for, but while we're here we might as well dance.

Belief is a truth held in the mind;
faith is a fire in the heart.

Everything has beauty, but not everyone sees it.

One of the most complicated tasks modern mankind faces is trying to figure out how to lead a simple life.

Do not work so hard to keep the outside presentable, it is the inside that really matters.

The trouble with reaching a crossroad in life is the lack of signposts.

Life is like a piano - what you get out of it depends on how you play it.

Peace of mind is not the absence of conflict from life, but the ability to cope with it.

The purpose of existence is not to make a living, but to make a life.

Three things make us content:
the seeing eye,
the hearing ear,
the responsive heart.

The thread that knits movement into a living pattern is change.

It's not so important where we are standing, but in what direction we are moving.

Imagination is more important than knowledge.

We all can't be shining examples, but we can all twinkle a little.

Life

Put a little more love in living, and you will love life more than ever before.

A task worth doing, and friends worth having, make life worthwhile.

What we must decide is how we are valuable
rather than how valuable we are.

Where we go hereafter depends on what we go after here.

Life is like an ever shifting kaleidoscope - a slight change and all patterns alter.

Good words and good deeds
keep life's garden free of weeds.

Life is a measure to be filled and not a cup to empty.

Life is like an escalator - you can move forward or backward, but you can not remain still.

It is a man that makes truth great,
not truth that makes man great.

What would life be if we had no courage to attempt?

Get your soul in tune with God before the concert begins.

The art of living lies in a fine mingling of letting go and holding on.

Get as much chocolate out of life as you can.

One of the wonders of life is the wonder of life.

The entire sum of existence is the magic of being needed by just one person.

There are no absolute answers to life - just revelations.

Some people are so busy being good they forget they should be busy doing good.

No person was ever honored for what he received; honor is the reward for what he gave.

Life is uncertain - eat dessert first.

The handsome gifts that fate and nature lend us, most often are the very ones that end us.

Life is like an onion - you peel it off one layer at a time, and sometimes it makes you weep.

Life is a flame that is always burning itself out, but it catches fire again every time a child is born.

Grief's best music is hope.

Far and away the best prize that life offers is the chance to work hard at work worth doing.

Every person's life is a fairy tale written by God's fingers.

Conceit may puff a man up, but never prop him up.

Life

Develop a passion for learning. If you do, you will never cease to grow.

Character is that which reveals moral purpose, exposing the class of things a man chooses or avoids.

Hope is a wish that won't go away.

Life is much like a vacation - we are so fixed on the idea of where we are going that we don't appreciate where we are.

Those who get the most out of life are those who don't ask much from it.

Life is a game - and it comes without instructions.

May you live as long as you want, and never want as long as you live.

Solitary people are never alone.

The only thing that one really knows about human nature is that it changes.

To truly live is the rarest thing in the world. Most people exist - that is all.

The perfection of man lies not in what a man has, but in what man is.

Life is a dance. Don't sit it out.

A secret of life is never to have an emotion that is unbecoming.

Life is never fair, and perhaps it is a good thing for most of us that it is not.

When one door is shut, another opens.

Miracles happen to those who believe in them.

The ten most powerful two-letter words are,
"If it is to be, it is up to me."

Change is inevitable, except from a vending machine.

Life is sexually transmitted.

Not everything that counts can be counted,
and not everything that can be counted counts.

Reality is, to a good extent, what we want it to be.

If you have accomplished all that you planned for your life, you have not planned enough.

Whatever your talent, use it in every way possible. Spend it lavishly like a billionaire intent on going broke.

One person with a dream is equal to ninety-nine who only have an interest.

Life is like a book - sometimes we must close one chapter and begin the next.

Life is not a spectacle or a feast; it is a predicament.

Life

The secret of life is not what happens to you,
but what you do with what happens to you.

Footprints on the sands of time are not made by sitting down.

Life is a work of art, designed by the one who lives it.

The greatest battles of life are fought out daily in the silent
chambers of the soul.

The deepest hunger of the human heart is to be understood.

If you don't run your own life, somebody else will.

Life is like a box of hand grenades - you never know what will
blow you to kingdom come.

Don't compromise yourself. You are all you have.

What is lovely never dies, but passes into loveliness.

Do it now. The future is promised to no one.

We promise according to our hopes,
and perform according to our fears.

To enjoy time alone, you must first appreciate the person you
are with.

The only way to have a life is to commit to it like crazy.

You can't shoplift from life. We don't get away with anything
we don't pay for.

Not what we gain, but what we give
measures the worth of the life we live.

It is not a tragedy to have only one talent. The tragedy is in not
using it.

We need to make the most of life each day before it flies away.

Your living is determined not so much by what life brings to
you, as by the attitude you bring to life.

The first step in anything new is having confidence in you.

There is only one corner of the universe you can be certain of
improving, and that is your own self.

The best helping hand that you will ever receive is the one at
the end of your own arm.

Life is like a ten-speed bike - we all have gears we never use.

Life is a bumpy road. What you need to do is develop good
shock absorbers.

The three F's: forgive, forget, and forge ahead.

Life is like a blind date - sometimes you need to have a little
faith.

Life is full of such sadness and sorrow. Some think it's better
not to be born at all, but how many have you met who were
that lucky?

The greatest of faults is to be conscious of none.

Life

The rule of life is to make business your pleasure, and pleasure your business.

Of all the diversions of life, there is none so proper to fill up its empty spaces as reading.

Life is like a taxi - the meter that keeps on ticking whether you are going anywhere or not.

The most important thing in every day life is absolute honesty; once you learn to fake that, life is a cinch.

It's not how long the row that matters - it's how you pick the beans.

A person starts to live when he can live outside himself.

Life's most persistent and urgent question is, "What are you doing for others?"

A man's life is painted with the colors of his imagination.

Our business in life is not to get ahead of others, but to get ahead of ourselves.

Your life might be the only bible some people ever read, so live accordingly.

Some people insist on going through life pushing all the doors marked 'pull'.

Life is too difficult to trust no one.

The important thing about your lot in life is whether you use it for parking or for building.

Learning to live is learning to let go.

Life is like a sandwich - the more you add to it, the better it becomes.

In the midst of everything,
take time to love and laugh and pray.
Then life will be worth living,
each and every day.

Life is like a shower - one wrong turn and you end up in hot water.

Don't let life discourage you. Everyone who got where he is, had to begin where he was.

Life is like a car - the slower you go, the longer you will last.

Sometimes in life, situations develop that only the half crazy can get out of.

It's bad enough to poke along, but it could be worse
to travel the road of life with gears stuck in reverse.

When life gives you lemons, make lemonade.
When life gives you scraps, make quilts.

One of life's little surprises is receiving mail with the rebate check you forgot.

Life

Put a little more into living, and you will love life more than ever before.

The simple things in life make living worthwhile - love and duty, work and rest, living close to nature.

Life is too short to remember slights and insults
to hold grudges that rob you of happiness
to waste time doing things that are of no value.

A pessimist is a person who is seasick during the entire voyage of life.

While traveling along the road of life, enjoy the journey and stop thinking about getting there.

Consideration for others is the basis of a good life.

Life is one long vacation to people who love their work.

Go confidently in the direction of your dreams, live life as you have always imagined.

A pessimist is a person who takes life with a grain of salt.

Look for the little things in life; a fish bone is much more dangerous than a soup bone.

The man who is getting the most out of life has already made ample provision for the worst.

If we want life to run smoothly, we must grease it with gratitude.

Good deeds are Certificates of Deposit invested in our future when the Book of Life is balanced.

If opportunity doesn't knock, build a door.

Life often pulls the rug out from under people who always demand the red carpet treatment.

Do not expect life to serve the dessert before you have eaten your veggies.

The capacity of receiving pleasure from common things is one of the secrets of a happy life.

As Confucius said, "Wherever you go, go with all your heart."

Think of life as a good book. The further you get into it, the more it begins to make sense.

Life is a long lesson in humility.

Truly appreciate those around you, and you will soon find many others around you.
Truly appreciate life, and you will find that you have more of it.

Wherever you go, no matter what the weather, always bring your own sunshine.

Most men's life is a contest between brains and glands.

The idea of life is to grab a little more happiness than destiny planned to give us.

Life

Nobody has a harder time going through life than the person who tries to take it soft.

Some of life's worst surprises are blessings in disguises.

When it comes to going after what you love in life, don't take no for an answer.

Times are different. Now the facts of life are about the birds and the bees. . . and the viruses.

Don't audit life. Show up and make the most of it now.

What folks say probably won't influence your life;
how you respond undoubtedly will.

It isn't life that matters, but the courage you bring to it.

If you can dance with adversity, you'll never be out of step with life.

People who have no respect for other forms of life usually have little respect for their own.

What greater evil could you wish a miser than long life?

The important moments in life are not the advertised ones, like birthdays or weddings, the real milestones come to the door of memory unannounced, like stray dogs that amble in, sniff around a bit, and simply never leave.

Life is like an exciting book, and every day starts a new chapter.

You cannot enjoy life without contributing to it.

A man who has work that suits him and a woman, whom he loves, has squared his accounts with life.

One of life's greatest crimes is theft of a child's trust.

Let him who would enjoy a good future waste none of his present.

What's the difference between school and life?
In school, you're taught a lesson and then given a test.
In life, you're given a test that teaches you a lesson.

Poor is the man who cannot enjoy the simple things of life.

Life is like a bridge - cross over it, but don't establish yourself upon it.

As long as you have a window, life is exciting.

Life for the European is a career; for the American, it is a hazard.

Each day of life is spent, and leaves the balance smaller.

Don't worry about the other fellow's life or you will be robbing yourself of your own.

Life is too short to waste time hating anyone.

May your life be like a snowflake - leave a mark, but not a stain.

Life

The best preparation for tomorrow is to give life your best today.

Nothing in life is to be feared. It is only to be understood.

Life is short; the present should be turned to profit with reasonableness and right.

Don't compare your life to others. You have no idea what their journey is all about.

I make the living, my mate makes the living worth while.

Keep your life and world inspired by staying in good company of friends and family.

Life is like college. Graduate well, and earn some honors.

Perhaps the secret of life is to run out of years before you run out of dreams.

To be successful in life, take everyone seriously except yourself.

If our lot in life is better, it is important to remember those who have gone before us to paved the way.

A routine usually holds your life together, but if it becomes too strong it can squeeze the life out of you.

In sports, winners don't ask for a replay, complain about the officiating or want to change the rules, the same is true in life.

If you want to live a happy life, tie it to a goal, not to people or objects.

The soul is born old, but grows young. That is the comedy of life.
The body is born young and grows old. That is the tragedy of life.

It's a shame that so many of the activities which make life enjoyable also make it shorter.

Reputation is made in a minute. Character is built in a lifetime.

By the time you learn all the lessons of life, you are too tired to walk to the head of the class.

After all this is over, all that will really have mattered is how we treated each other.

Three little words can sum up life.
It goes on.

Seeing death as the end of life is like seeing the horizon as the end of the ocean.

The greatest thing in life is to be needed

A life that touches the hearts of others goes on forever.

Time

Time

We do not remember days - we remember moments.

Nothing is as far away as one minute ago.

Half our life is spent trying to find something to do with the time we have rushed through life trying to save.

When the time of need arises, the time for planning has passed.

With every rising of the sun,
think of life as just begun.

If only we could think twice and still be in the conversation.

Be interested in the future, because you're going to spend the rest of your life there.

I'm not afraid of tomorrow, for I have seen yesterday and I love today.

No day is wasted if it makes a memory.

Everyday is an opportunity to do something you've never done before.

Time is the coin of your life. It is the only coin you have, and only you can determine how it will be spent. Be careful lest you let other people spend it for you.

Don't use time or words carelessly. Neither can be retrieved.

Lose an hour in the morning and you will be all day hunting it.

How you spend your time is more important than how you spend your money. Money mistakes can be corrected, but time is gone forever.

One of the greatest enemies we can ever face is the illusion that there will be more time tomorrow than today.

You can't build a reputation on what you are going to do.

The trouble with time is that you don't learn to make the most of it until most of it is gone.

Dreams come true for those who don't oversleep.

A true procrastinator is one who puts off until tomorrow what has already been put off until today.

A timely present for an always tardy person is an alarm clock.

There is a time to speak your mind and a time to mind your speech.

It is difficult to live in the present,
ridiculous to live in the future, and
impossible to live in the past.

How long a minute is depends on which side of the bathroom door you're on.

Time

Today is a smooth white seashell, hold it close and listen to the beauty of the hours.

For every minute of action, there should be an hour of thought.

Sixty seconds of being happy are lost every minute you are angry.

Nothing in the world arouses more false hopes than the first four hours of a day.

An optimist is a person who leaves the dishes, because he thinks he will feel more like doing them in the morning.

When the sun goes down let it take the day's troubles with it.

Until you value yourself, you will not value your time. Until you value your time, you will not do anything with it.

Regret demands payment of your time, but renders you no service.

Procrastination is the art of keeping up with yesterday.

The sunrise never finds us where the sunset left us.

People spend so much time worrying about what they did yesterday and dreading what might happen tomorrow, they miss out on all of their todays.

You may not be able to turn back the clock, but you can always wind it up again.

Yesterday is history.
Tomorrow is a mystery.
Today is a gift.
That's why it's called: The Present.

There is no such thing in anyone's life as an unimportant day.

There is no royal road to anything. One thing at a time, and all things in succession.

That which grows slowly endures.

Today is the tomorrow you worried about yesterday.

When we take time to slow down, pause, and pray,
we seem to end up with a better day.

Lost time is never found again.

An old belief is like an old shoe. We so value its comfort that we fail to notice the hole in it.

Our worst misfortunes never happen, and most miseries lie in anticipation.

Take rest; a field that has rested gives a bountiful crop.

Everything cometh to he who waiteth, as long as he who waiteth works like hell while he waiteth.

Why is there no expiration date on sour cream?

The future belongs to those who believe in the beauty of their dreams.

Time

If you are patient in one moment of anger, you will escape a hundred days of sorrow.

I don't like Fridays - they're to close to Mondays.

Worry pulls tomorrow's cloud over today's sunshine.

Tradition is what once was a bright new idea.

It's not too late to run away and join the circus.

The only limits to our realization of tomorrow will be our doubts of today.

Procrastination is a habit that most of us are going to break - tomorrow.

The only time you should procrastinate is when you think you should get even with somebody.

Gossip travels with the speed of delight.

Every year it seems to take less time to fly across the ocean and longer to drive to work.

Trying times are not the time to stop trying.

Everything is relative. Years ago, women thought that the washboard was a great technological advancement compared to pounding clothes on a rock.

If pleasures are greatest in anticipation, just remember that this is also true of trouble.

Three enemies of personal peace:
Regret over yesterday's mistakes;
Anxiety over tomorrow's problems;
Ingratitude for today's blessings.

Retirees think each week has six Saturdays, then Sunday. My brother thinks there are seven Saturdays.

Every passing day is one that is gone forever, make sure it is one in which you have done something for others, especially those who cannot do for themselves.

We cannot alter the past, but we can be alert for the future.

When we consider when to begin, it becomes too late.

The trouble with traveling in the fast lane is that you get to the other end in a hurry.

Lost, somewhere between sunrise and sunset, 60 golden minutes, each set with 60 diamond seconds. No reward is offered, for they are gone forever.

It's not too difficult to acquire the habit of punctuality; it's just a matter of time.

The best preparation for tomorrow is doing your best today.

One trouble with most of us is that we spend too much of our present planning how to spend our future.

The time to mind somebody else's business is when he doesn't.

Procrastination is opportunity's natural assassin.

Time

I have always been in the right place at the right time. Of course, I steered myself there.

Don't think everyone is a Sunday driver. It might be a Friday driver still looking for a place to park.

No man is to be pitied except the one whose future lies behind.

Life is too short to waste time complaining about how short it is.

Nothing makes you realize how precious time is until you pay a parking garage fee.

Do not put off until tomorrow what you can do today - tomorrow there may he a law against it.

Time spent trying to get even is better used trying to get ahead.

Being an accomplished worrier makes today's problems seem trivial compared to what you imagine will go wrong tomorrow.

Too many people think the speed of light gets here much too early in the morning.

Sometimes I wonder why people knock themselves out to always be on time. Usually there is no one present to appreciate it.

Spend each day as if it was your last and you will be broke by sunset.

Anger is the only thing to put off until tomorrow.

Spring is nature's way of saying, "Let's Party!"

Tomorrow is a dream romance.
Today is a lover to enjoy.

Every day is a gift, so don't rap it.

The only limit to our realization of tomorrow will be our doubts of today.

The present is colored by the past, but we can choose the colors of the future.

Live today as though you were going to die tomorrow and have to answer for it.

If you live by the calendar, your days are numbered.

Mondays are a hard way to spend one seventh of your life.

You can discover more about a person in an hour of play than in a year of conversation.

Try to make at least one person smile today.

It is well to be up before daybreak, for such habits contribute to health, wealth, and wisdom.

Every age is modern to those who are living it.

Peace is seeing a sunset and knowing who to thank.

If you learn something new every day, the days are not wasted.

Time

The bad news is that time flies, the good news is that you are the pilot.

Spring is when you feel like whistling, even with a shoe full of slush.

A person lost in his work has probably found his future.

A guest sees more in an hour than a host sees in a year.

Impatience is waiting in a hurry.

The chief worries of life arise from the foolish habit of looking before and after.

You can't get much done by starting tomorrow.

Sunset in one land is sunrise in another.

To live long, live slowly.

Don't let the future scare you, it is as uncertain as you are.

A sign in a small town has to be admired for its cynical honesty, "Antique tables made daily."

It's only when the tide goes out that you learn who's been swimming naked.

You can spend it any way you wish, but you can spend it only once.

Plant a tree to live in the faraway future.

May is nature's way of apologizing for February.

We can improve our tomorrows with a better understanding of our yesterdays.

Be not afraid of moving slowly: be afraid of standing still.

In summer, the song sings itself.

Each day comes bearing gifts - it's up to you to untie the ribbons.

The past always looks better than it was, because it isn't here.

The day the Lord created hope was probably the same day he created Spring.

Get a good night's sleep; things will look better in the morning.

It's easy enough to be pleasant when life goes by like a song, but the man worthwhile is the man who can smile after everything else goes wrong.

There's a first time for everything.

I have more time than money, and sharing time with others is what life is all about.

It takes one hand to do dishes today, tomorrow it will take two.

If you have time to do it over, you have time to do it right.

Time

Nobody will know how long it took you to do this; all they will know is what it looks like when you are done.

No matter how busy you are, you owe yourself at least enough time out of each day to read.

Those who make the worst use of their time are the first to complain of its brevity.

Do nothing hastily, but catching of fleas.

To perfect the character; live each day as if the last.

Time and tide wait for no man.

Make it a point to do something every day that you don't want to do. This is the golden rule for acquiring the habit of doing your duty without pain.

It is never too late to give up our prejudices.

One of the problems with living for the moment is that a moment doesn't last very long.

The key to success is setting aside eight hours a day for work and eight hours for sleep, and making sure they are not the same hours.

Don't borrow trouble from tomorrow, tomorrow will take care of itself.

Let's not cross that bridge until we come to it.

To choose time is to save time.

You cannot do a kindness too soon, for you never know how soon it will be too late.

A man who dares to waste one hour of time has not discovered the value of life.

Worrying does not empty tomorrow of its troubles, it empties today of its strength.

Don't do everything today. Save some mistakes for tomorrow.

Prayer is too often like a lamp that isn't used until it gets dark.

Few things have a shorter life than a clean garage.

We will never enter much in our journal of accomplishment if we always wait for the right time to do anything.

Many people worry a lot today about tomorrow, because they didn't worry a little yesterday about today.

Yesterday's sin is today's lifestyle.

The past gives us experience and memories;
the present gives us challenges and opportunities;
the future gives us vision and hope.

The years teach much which the days never know.

A weatherman tells you today what is going to happen tomorrow and then the next day explains why it didn't.

The best time to do something worthwhile is between yesterday and tomorrow.

Time

Promise yourself more moments like this.

The way each day will look to you all starts with who you are looking to.

Today is the first day of the rest of your life, but relax, so is tomorrow!

Why worry about tomorrow? Who knows what will hit you today?

Let not the mistakes of yesterday or the fears of tomorrow spoil today.

Winter is the time we try to keep the house as warm as it was in summer when we complained about it.

Summer is the time we try to keep the house as cold as it was in the winter when we complained about it.

I like time clocks. After a really bad day, it's nice to have something to punch.

Memories are keepsakes of the happy times we have known.

A good snapshot stops a moment from running away.

The future belongs to those who create it.

April puts a spirit of youth in everything.

Time is like a circus, always packing up and moving away.

Delay is the deadliest form of denial.

To be quite oneself, one must first waste a little time.

They talk of the dignity of work. The dignity is in leisure.

Prediction is very difficult, especially about the future.

Truth has no special time of its own. Its hour is now - always.

Nothing makes a person more productive than the lost minute.

Everything takes longer than you expect.

The time is always right to do what is right.

Spend the afternoon. You can't take it with you.

I stopped whining about not having enough time when I realized that we all have 24 hours a day.

It is never too late to be <u>what</u> you might have been.
It is never too late to be <u>who</u> you might have been.

Our life is made entirely of moments multiplied.

Strike while the iron is hot.

We often get in quicker by the back door than by the front.

Start doing today what you wish to do well tomorrow.

Time

A minute is a little thing, but minutes make the day.
So crowd in some kind deeds before it slips away.

If you wait, there will come nectarlike fair weather.

The days are too short and the nights aren't long enough.

Timely good deeds are nicer than afterthoughts.

Daylight Savings Time is like cutting off one end of a blanket
and sewing it on the other end.

There should be a better reward for promptness than having to
wait for everyone else.

There won't be time to dwell in the past if we keep busy today.

Don't let the urgent crowd out the important.

Nostalgia is the sandpaper that removes the rough edges from
the good old days.

Worried about tomorrow? You did that yesterday about today.

Setting a good example for the children takes all of the fun out
of middle age.

Spring is the time when youth dreams and old age remembers.

'In the nick of time' is an expression invented by a man who
overslept one morning and had to shave in a hurry.

Blessed is the person who is too busy to worry in the daytime and too sleepy to worry at night.

The best thing about spring is that it comes when it is most needed.

At the beginning of the year, we have another chance to carve a beautiful shape in our own landscape.

Worry is today's mouse eating tomorrow's cheese.

It's not how many hours you put in, but what you put into the hours that count.

Don't trouble trouble, till it troubles you.

You're only cooking up trouble when you stew about tomorrow.

We all need time alone: to think, to dream, to wonder.

Sleep on what you plan to do. Don't stay awake over what you have done.

At the rate changes are occurring everywhere, anyone nostalgic for the "good old days" is yearning for last week.

The time to relax is when we don't have the time.

The man of the hour is the person who rarely watches the clock.

Don't you love those winter mornings when you don't have to get up at the crack of dawn to see the sunrise?

Time

Moments are like little pockets of time crammed with all of life's possibilities.

Today turns a new page in the history of your life.

The best eraser in the world is a good night's sleep.

The worst of all thieves is the one who steals your time.

A person who took yesterday and planned for tomorrow is enjoying it today.

Time can wash away personal dirt, but stains must wear off.

Do you realize that tomorrow people will refer to today as 'the good old days'?

I don't mind being a procrastinator. In fact, I should have started sooner.

Always put off until tomorrow what you shouldn't do at all.

I wouldn't mind the rat race so much if there was more cheese to go around.

You never realize how short a month is until you start to pay alimony.

The moment may be temporary, but the memory is forever.

One thing worse than forgetfulness is remembering things that never happened.

Some days are a total waste of makeup.

If it wasn't for Monday mornings, Friday nights just wouldn't be the same.

Night falls, but never breaks and
day breaks, and never falls.

Opportunity is not a lengthy visitor.

May each new day inspire you with peace and hope.

Memory is the diary we carry with us.

You can clutch the past so tightly that it leaves your arms too full to embrace the present.

Recall it as often as you wish. . . a happy memory never wears out.

Do your best today and tomorrow will be easier.

We are all part of the same story, as long as one of us is still around to remember.

Past experience should be a guidepost, not a hitching post.

A true test of patience is not minding being put on hold.

Most people spend a lot of time dreaming about the future, never realizing a little arrives each day.

Time

Today might not be so good, but tomorrow you get another chance to get it right.

You never know when you're making a memory.

An early morning walk is a blessing for the whole day.

Dream as if you will live forever,
live as if you will die today.

Forget the troubles that passed away, but remember the blessings that come each day.

Today is the day to make memories.

We cannot lose our faith in the future without first losing our memory of the past.

Don't let yesterday use up too much of today.

If you thought you were going to die tomorrow you would know how to live today.

You will always find time for that which you place first.

The best thing about the future is that it only comes one day at a time.

Every man is the architect of his own future.

Even if I knew the world was going to end tomorrow, I would plant a tree today.

We can improve our tomorrows with a better understanding of our yesterdays.

To better the future, know the past.

Sleep is like air - it doesn't seem all that important until you're not getting any.

Time is the wages of life; invest it, don't spend it.

Take a lesson from the clock - it passes time by keeping its hands busy.

This only is denied the gods: the power to remake the past.

Instead of counting the days, make the days count.

If you hem in both ends of your day with prayer, it won't be so likely to unravel in the middle.

Don't put off enjoyment - there's no time like the present.

You can always recall moving an item to a safer place, but never recall where that place is.

God made time, but man made haste.

I know not what the future holds, but I know who holds the future.

The average human heart beats 100,000 times a day. Make those beats count.

Time

The trees that are slow to grow bear the best fruit.

No day is so bad it can't be fixed with a nap.

One never knows what each day is going to bring. The important thing is to be open and ready for it.

Autumn is a second Spring when every leaf is a flower.

There is no such thing in anyone's life as an unimportant day.

The trouble with making mental notes is that the ink fades so fast.

There are seven ways to warm your feet in February. Dipping them in the Caribbean is one. If you can afford that, forget the other six.

Do it tomorrow - you have made enough mistakes today.

August is that time of year when you go to turn on the air conditioner and it already is.

Most problems can be solved in less time than time spent worrying about them.

Time is not measured by years that we live,
but by the deeds that we do
and the joys that we give.

Today's tendency is tomorrow's custom.

If you have something to say, to do, or to write, do it today, for in life there is not always a second chance.

The longer you keep your temper the more it will improve.

Spring - when Mother Nature begins to liquidate her frozen assets.

When April rains come; some people see only puddles, while others see flowers.

Nothing is as dangerous as being too modern. One is apt to grow old-fashioned quite suddenly.

People who wouldn't think of wasting money, squander time away each day.

Save the good times in your memory bank. There will come a day when you will want to start making withdrawals.

Nothing beats uncertainty, to make tomorrow more interesting.

Time is something that goes by slowly between paydays.

Tomorrow does not belong to you. Do it today.

The measure of life is not its duration, but its donation.

Whatever old way you don't want to change was once the new way.

It takes most of an hour to look one's best.
It takes most of a lifetime to be one's best.

The future has a way of arriving unannounced.

Time

The only difference between the saint and the sinner is that every saint has a past, and every sinner has a future.

Tomorrow is often the busiest day of the week.

If you don't think every day is a good day, try missing one.

The amount of sleep required by the average person is about ten minutes more.

Time is what keeps everything from happening at once.

It's not the pace of life that concerns me, it's the sudden stop at the end.

The first hour of waking is the rudder that guides the whole day.

Time is a dressmaker specializing in alterations.

Waste of time is the most extravagant and costly of all expenses.

Time spent with friends and family is time worth remembering.

I plan to be spontaneous, tomorrow.

Time is a river without banks.

Lost wealth may be replaced by industry,
lost knowledge by study,
lost health by temperance or medicine, but
lost time is gone forever.

Despair is a foolish squandering of precious time.

There is definitely an energy crisis. It's called Monday morning.

Some weeks you really need Saturday on a Wednesday.

Time flies - Spend it with people who mean the most to you.

Don't worry, the future comes soon enough.

To look back all the time is boring, excitement lies in tomorrow.

A grouch is a person who somehow can manage to find something wrong with even the good old days.

Eat one live toad in the morning, and nothing worse will happen to you the rest of the day.

If it wasn't for the last minute, nothing would get done.

All the gardens of yesterdays are in the roots of the past. All the flowers of our tomorrows are in the seeds of today.

Worry is wasting today's time and cluttering up tomorrow's opportunities with yesterday's troubles.

History swings from left to right through time; it never walks a straight line.

Gratitude is the memory of the heart.

Time

The glory of the past is an illusion. So is the glory of the future.

Nostalgia is like a grammar lesson - you find the present tense and the past perfect.

Time and wilted salad wait for no man.

Nostalgia never gets old.

There's no time like the present.

How we spend our days is, of course, how we spend our lives.

May you look back on the past with as much pleasure as you look forward to the future.

Prayer should be the key to the day
and the lock of the night.

"Merry" is a word for Christmas.
"Happy" is a word for New Year's.
"Thanks" is a word for all year long.

No one can go back and make a brand new start, but anyone can start from now and make a brand new end.

Take time:
to work - it is the price of success;
to think - it is the source of power;
to play - it is the secret of perpetual youth;
to read - it is the foundation of wisdom;
to worship - it is the highway to reverence;
to be friendly - it is the road to happiness;
to dream - it is hitching your wagon to a star.

One of your greatest possessions is the 24 hours directly ahead of you.

Don't worry too much about today, tomorrow it will be yesterday and there is no sense in worrying about the past.

If you believe that the past can't be changed, you haven't read a celebrity's autobiography.

Our days are like identical suitcases, all the same size,
but some people can pack more into them than others.

Regrets over yesterday and the fear of tomorrow are twin thieves that rob us of the moment.

I wish I could stand on a busy corner, hat in hand, and beg people to throw me all their wasted hours.

A minute of action is better than an hour of worry.

Real generosity towards the future lies in giving all to the present.

The one duty we owe to history is to rewrite it.

What the future has in store for you depends on what you have stored for the future.

Time is the most valuable thing a man can spend.

The end isn't always where it should be.

Time

Ageing

To stay youthful, stay useful.

A good memory should be a sieve - the sand should go through and only the best nuggets be retained.

If things get better with age, then I am magnificent.

When you get up and go has got up and gone, you have reached old age.

The longer one lives, the more beautiful life becomes.

This is the final test of a gentleman: his respect for those who can no longer be of possible value to him.

Age and treachery will always overcome youth and skill. Conniving and brilliance only come with age and experience.

Ageing seems to be the only available way to live a long life.

Years may wrinkle the skin, but to give up enthusiasm wrinkles the soul.

What most consider as virtue, after the age of fifty is simply a loss of energy.

Age does not depend upon years, but upon temperament and health. Some men are born old, and some never grow so.

Ageing

We get too soon old, and too late smart.

We have put more effort into helping folks reach old age than into helping them enjoy it.

The older the violin, the sweeter the music.

No matter how old you are, there's always something good to look forward to.

To remain young while growing old is the highest blessing.

The more sand that has escaped from the hourglass of our life, the clearer we should see through it.

Ageing would be easier if the appetite failed as often as the digestive system.

One generation plants trees and the next enjoys the shade.

Age does not diminish the extreme disappointment of having a scoop of ice cream fall from the cone.

The first 40 years of life give us the text; the next 40 provide the commentary.

Youth is a function of living, but age is a work of art.

The excitement of learning separates youth from old age. As long as you are learning, you are not old.

Old age is like a rocket launching - at a certain stage, you count down.

The latter part of a wise man's life is taken up in curing all of the follies, prejudices, and false opinions he has contracted in the former part.

Do not resent growing old, many are denied the privilege.

As you age, people may forget what you said, but they will never forget how you made them feel.

The surprising thing about young fools is how many survive to become old fools.

For the first half of life, people tell you what you should do; for the second half, they tell you what you should have done.

Middle age is having a choice between two temptations and choosing the one that will get you home earlier.

You are young only once, but you can stay immature for life.

The spiritual eyesight improves as the physical eyesight declines.

The ageing process has you firmly in its grasp if you never get the urge to throw a snowball.

The minute a man ceases to grow, no matter what his years, he begins to be old.

He who is of calm and happy nature will hardly feel the pressure of age, but to him who is of an opposite disposition, youth and age are equally a burden.

Ageing

The wiser mind mourns less for what age takes away than what it leaves behind.

Children are the only people wise enough to enjoy today, without regretting yesterday or fearing tomorrow.

You can only perceive real beauty in a person as they get older.

As people grow older, they pay less attention to what men say and watch what they do.

The excess of our youth are checks written against our age and they are payable with interest thirty years later.

Old age is like everything else. To make a success of it, you have to start young.

To triumph over old age, be hopeful, kind, cheerful, and reverent, and keep the heart unwrinkled.

You are young and useful at any age if you are still planning for tomorrow.

A heart in love with beauty never grows old.

How old are you madam?
I'm approaching forty.
From which direction?

Age is a matter of the mind; if you don't mind, it doesn't matter.

Nostalgia is the vice of the aged.

We do not count a man's years, until he has nothing else to count.

Intellectual blemishes, like facial ones, grow more prominent with age.

The gardener's rule applies to youth and age:
When young, sow wild oats,
but when old, grow sage.

To have been loved, you grow old beautifully.

At my age, getting lucky is finding my car in the parking lot.

No wise man ever wished to be younger.

In youth we run into difficulties;
in old age difficulties run into us.

Wisdom does not automatically come with old age. Nothing does - except wrinkles.

Some wines improve with age, but only if the grapes were good to start.

Your thinking is OK until you start hiding your own Easter eggs.

To dream is to be ageless.

A society grows great when old men plant trees, whose shade they shall never sit in.

Ageing

It is not true that people stop pursuing dreams because they grow old, they grow old because they stop pursuing dreams.

Grow up as soon as you can, it pays. The only time you really live fully is from 40 to 70.

Age should direct its efforts more to preparing youth for the path and less to preparing the path for youth.

Middle age is when your age starts to show around your middle.

One of the annoying disadvantages of maturity is now you really are old enough to know better.

XL is the Roman numeral for 40. . . Hmm.

I'm not afraid to die. I just don't want to be there when it happens.

Some people spend the first half of their lives indulging in excesses that shorten the last half.

The first half of life consists of the capacity to enjoy without the chance;
the last half consists of the chance without the capacity.

Old men dream dreams - young men see visions.

If you wait until retirement to start living, you have waited too long.

Profundity of thought belongs to youth,
clarity of thought to old age.

To men over forty, don't worry about losing hair; think of it as gaining face.

Longevity can be Hell, knowing things will inevitably go bad, but not knowing when.

Man must live long, to see how short life is.

When you are forty, half of you belongs to the past, and when you are seventy, nearly all of you does.

The secret of staying young is to live honestly, eat slowly, and lie about your age.

One can't help getting older, but one doesn't have to be old.

Everything else you grow out of, but you never recover from childhood.

Young men want to be faithful, and are not.
Old men want to be faithless, and cannot.

The thing about being dead is that there's no future in it.

If you want pleasant memories, you need to arrange for them in advance.

At twenty we worry about what others think of us;
at forty we don't care about what others think of us;
at sixty we discover they haven't been thinking about us at all.

One thing about new technology I like - it grows old faster than I do.

Ageing

How old would you be if you didn't know how old you are?

She looked like she had been picked up by the heels and dipped in age.

Morning is the time of day when the retiring generation is rising and the rising generation is retiring.

Young at heart; slightly older in other places.

The age of a person doesn't mean a thing. The best tunes are played on the oldest fiddles.

Be a man easy in your skin.

Genius has no youth, but starts with the ripeness of age and experience.

At my age I have seen it all, have heard it all, and have done it all, but I just can't remember it all.

It's hard to judge the age of a person whose spirit has remained young.

Age wrinkles the body.
Quitting wrinkles the soul.

Old age is always fifteen years older than I am.

In old age you spend half of your time looking for a bathroom, and the other half trying to remember people's names.

At my age I can't see the forest or the trees.

The trouble with class reunions is that old flames have become even older.

Age is just a number and I keep it unlisted.

To be seventy years young is far more cheerful than to be forty years old.

The trick is to live a long time without growing old.

At 20 years of age the will reigns,
at 30 the wit,
at 40 the judgment.

To get back one's youth, one has merely to repeat one's follies.

After you retire, you spend half your time looking for things you lose.

An old-timer is a person who has had many interesting experiences, some of them true.

Wrinkled was not one of the things I wanted to be when I grew up.

Age is not important, unless you are cheese or wine.

Middle age is that transition period between 'pinch an inch' and 'grab some flab'.

As soon as people are old enough to know better, they don't know anything at all.

Ageing

We live our lives forward, but understand them backward.

Age appears to be best in four things,
old wood best to burn,
old wine to drink,
old friends to trust,
and old authors to read.

If you pull out a gray hair, seven will come to its funeral.

Spring is the time the youth dreams and old age remembers.

You know you're getting old when the candles cost more than the cake.

Being 'over the hill' isn't so bad if the descent isn't too rapid.

Anyone observant enough to guess your age will annoy you in other ways, too.

Men over seventy offer one the devotion of a lifetime.

One's past is what one is. It is the only way by which people should be judged.

At the end of your days, be leaning forward, not falling backward.

People are like wine - some turn to vinegar, but the best improve with age.

Some people are slow to change their minds. Ask their age and they will give the same answer for years.

You are older when what was called adventure is now called stress.

We should resolve to be more understanding of the very young, old, weak, and sick. Sometime in life you will have been all of them.

One of the secrets of a long and fruitful life is to forgive everybody everything, every night before you go to bed.

As people grow older, they discover that most of the things they worry about never happen.

You can often tell what makes a person tick by how he unwinds.

Most people say when you get old, you have to give things up. I say you get old, because you give things up.

Age is kind only to those who do not hate it.

You are getting old when you are ready, willing, and able, but not at the same time.

Sometimes gray hair isn't premature.

Old age is when you always have something to live with or something to live without.

People who see beauty never grow old.

You know you are getting old when you know your way around, but don't feel like going.

Ageing

To truly appreciate the dignity and beauty in an old face, you have to read between the lines.

Whatever poet, orator, or sage may say of it, old age is still old age.

Every young man should know well at least one old man to whom he can go when he wants the teachings of experience rather than mere sympathy.

An old gentleman in a nursing home was reading his Bible. A visitor came along and asked him what he was doing. "Cramming for my final," he replied.

Don't count your years as they mount. Instead do everything to make them count.

Youth is when life is filled with thrills. Old age is when you are filled with pills.

Don't worry about avoiding temptation. As you grow older, it will avoid you.

An old timer is some one who remembers when safe sex meant your parents had gone away for the weekend.

Be life long or short, its completeness depends on what it was lived for.

None are as old as those who have outlived enthusiasm.

Many of us feel that we would like to return to the good old days; of course, we would want to take television, air-conditioning, and our higher wages with us.

Regrets are the natural property of gray hairs.

As people grow older, one of the things that makes them happy about putting on old clothes is that they can.

Old age begins the moment you trade in your dreams for memories.

It is less painful to learn in youth than to be ignorant in age.

Raising the retirement age is like moving the finish line when the horses are coming down the homestretch.

You know you are getting old when you go duck hunting just to please the dog.

You know that it's middle-age when you feel every morning the way you used to feel, when you were coming down with something.

There is no sadder sight than immaturity grown to an old age.

Birthdays are such happy times. It's too bad they come on the same day you get another day older.

What we are when we are old is what we learned when we were young.

Time tells on a person, especially a good time.

The old age of an eagle is better than the youth of a sparrow.

You are not old until it takes you longer to rest than it does to get tired.

Ageing

Experience is a great advantage; the problem is that when you get the experience you are too old to do anything about it.

A person's age can be measured by the degree of pain he feels as he comes in contact with a new idea.

Middle age is the awkward period when father time starts catching up with Mother Nature.

Too many people long for immortality, but don't know what to do with themselves on a rainy afternoon.

When you depart, leave a vacuum, not a wake.

You are getting old when you are doing more and more things for the last time, and fewer and fewer things for the first time.

Inside every seventy year old is a teenager asking, "What happened?"

I always wanted to be the last man on earth just to see if all those women were lying to me.

When an old person dies, a library is lost.

Happiness is not to look your age.
Ecstasy is not to feel your age.

It is the fight itself that keeps you young.

When your friends begin to flatter you on how young you look, it's a sure sign you are getting old.

Maturity begins when we are content to feel we are right about something without feeling the necessity to prove someone else is wrong.

Retirement has nothing to do with doing nothing.

What is catastrophic for the young is mildly troubling to the old.

My wife asked me what I was going to do today.
I told her, "Nothing."
She said, "You did that yesterday."
I replied, "I haven't finished."

The harvest of old age is the abundance of blessings previously secured.

If you can't become mean, nasty, and grumpy, what's the point of growing old?

A man does not become mature. He just gives up habits.

Why is it that any person your own age always looks older than you do?

Common sense is the collection of prejudices acquired by age eighteen.

At middle age the soul should be opening up like a rose, not closing up like a cabbage.

A class reunion is a gathering where you come to the conclusion that most of the people your own age are a lot older than you are.

Ageing

Maturity consists of mellowing with the years and growing old gratefully.

Nature gives you the face you have at twenty. It is up to you to merit the face you have at fifty.

When you are young, you watch people.
When you are mature, you watch out for people.

Progress is the victory of imagination over the status quo, The telling sign of old age is not caring anymore.

The frightening thing about middle age is knowing you will grow out of it.

What we keep in memory is ours to get better with age.

Good grooming and smart clothing may take years off a person's age, but you can't fool a flight of stairs.

About the only thing that comes without effort is old age.

If you wait too long to get your life on the right track, you may find out that the train has already left.

Growing older isn't upsetting, being perceived as old is.

Old is when you have an achy, breaky everything.

You are growing old gracefully when the number of things you can no longer do is roughly equal to the number of things you no longer want to do.

Retirees know it all and have plenty of time to tell you about it.

Youth is when we are always hunting greener pastures, and middle age is when we can barely mow the one we have.

Formula for youth: Keep your enthusiasm and forget your birthdays.

'Over the hill' means the hardest climb is over and the view is terrific.

Middle age is that time in life, if your clothes don't fit, then it's you who needs the alterations.

Old age should be regarded as a reward for a lifetime of hard work, but it can only be a punishment if one insists on doing the same things one has always done, measuring present achievements by past ones and inevitably falling short.

It takes time to grow old, and I have never had any.

Retirement is when you reach an age when you still have a first-class mind, but your body is going tourist.

There is no better way to fight old age than by refusing to act the part.

One thing I've learned in growing old, no doubt you've noticed too.
The kids to whom you gave advice, now give advice to you.

Age is a very high price to pay for maturity and maturity is a high price to pay for growing up.

Ageing

Growing old beats the alternative - dying young.

Middle age is when you finally get your head together just in time to watch your body fall apart.

Cherish all your happy moments; they make a fine cushion for old age.

People 65 and older memorize their social security numbers.
Those 35 to 65 remember their credit card numbers.
Those 15 and under know cable channel numbers.

The older a person gets, the farther he had to walk to school as a child.

People do not stop doing things because they get older.
They get older because they stop doing things.

Whatever makes me tick needs winding.

The first big shock of retirement is when you realize there are no days off.

You are not too old if you prefer dates to prunes.

Look at the bright side: No matter how old you are - you are younger than you will ever be again.

Growing old is inevitable.
Growing up is optional.

Enthusiasm is what enables some folks to die of old age without being old.

No one is ever as old as he hopes to be.

The secret of staying young is being too busy to think about it.

Nothing ages a person faster than trying to prove he is still as young as ever.

When we are young we want to change the world:
When we are old we want to change the young.

One of the advantages of being young is that you don't let common sense get in the way of doing things that everybody knows are impossible.

Everyone wants to live long, but no one wants to grow old.

Youth has no age.

Many people get older so much faster than they grow up.

We are of a generation that went from outdoor plumbing to indoor swimming in one generation.

Getting old is fascinating. The older you get, the older you want to get.

Strive to die young at a very old age.

When you win, you are an old pro,
when you lose you are an old man.

You can take no credit for beauty at 16, but if you are beautiful at 60, it will be your soul's own doing.

Ageing

Too many people die at thirty and aren't buried until they are seventy-five.

Forty is the old age of youth.
Fifty is the youth of old age.

It's not that age brings childhood back again; age merely shows what children we remain.

In the end it's not the years in your life that count.
It's the life in your years.

He is about a year from retirement, but his brain retired ten years ago.

God put me on earth to accomplish a certain number of things.
Right now I'm so far behind, I will never die.

He who is deaf, dumb, and blind will live a hundred years in peace.

Why can't life's problems hit us when we are a teenager and know all the answers?

The great thing about getting older is that you don't lose all the other ages you have been.

"Do you know when you are getting old?"
"I give up."

You are only young once, but you can be immature all your life.

Decide to live forever or die in the attempt.

Experience enables you to recognize a mistake when you make it again.

Don't part with your dreams. When they are gone, you may still exist, but you have ceased to live.

The only thing that doesn't slow down as you get older is the rate at which everything slows down.

Each person is born to one possession, which out values all his others - his last breath.

Sex after ninety is like trying to shoot pool with a rope.

Crossing the street in New York keeps old people young, if they make it.

A wise man learns from the mistakes of others. Nobody lives long enough to make them all himself.

Growing old is only a state of mind brought on by gray hair, false teeth, wrinkles, a big belly, shortness of breath, and being constantly pooped.

Nothing keeps a heart feeling young than looking at the world through the eyes of a child.

You are getting old when you stoop to tie your shoes and wonder what else you can do while you're down there.

The trouble with being young is that you are not old enough to enjoy it.

The going gets easier when you are over the hill.

Ageing

You know you are ageing if you get lost strolling down Memory Lane.

Youth looks ahead,
old age looks back
and middle age looks tired.

You are never too old to learn and never too young to know it all.

The best way to tell a lady's age is not to.

A man doesn't just grow old.
He becomes old by not growing.

It's not the number of years that makes you old, but the idea that you are getting old.

Once you're over the hill you begin to pick up speed.

To worry about your age is silly, Every time you're a year older so is everyone else.

Nothing really makes the younger generation seem so bad as having lost your membership in it.

Midlife crisis is that moment when you realize your children and your clothes are about the same age.

When you are young, try to be realistic; as you get older, become idealistic and you will live longer.

Old age is when your favorite theme park is slumberland.

Some men defy old age. They still believe that they as good as they never were.

Social Security has done more than anything else to make people admit their correct age.

When pointing to another's past, remember it is his history - not his destiny.

Middle age begins when you become more interested in how long a car will last rather than how fast it goes.

It's nice to know that no matter how many birthdays you have, you are never as old as your children think you are.

Age is important only in dead fish and good wine.

Ever notice that as you get older the days get longer, but the years shorter?

At your 25th class reunion, you wear a name tag so your classmates can remember who you are.
At your 50th reunion, you wear one so you can remember who you are.

In youth we learn, in old age we understand.

The man who is a pessimist before 50 knows too much; if he is an optimist after that, he knows too little.

Never tell your sister-in-law's age.

You are mature when you know what is foolhardy and what is courage.

Ageing

Old age is when you buy a birthday cake and the baker throws in a smoke alarm for free.

The young have aspirations that never come to pass.
The old have memories of what never happened.

You've been around for quite some time if you remember when the first person an accident victim asked for was a doctor, not a lawyer.

It is all relative, to a five-year old, a ten-year old is a senior citizen.

It takes only a moment to hug a child, but a lifetime is too short for him to forget it.

You can't control the length of your life, but you can control the breadth and depth.

Education is the best provision for old age.

The memories we collect and give
brighten our lives as long as we live.

Remember the years, but forget the tears.

Gray hairs are a glorious crown, which is worn by a righteous life.

A man is not old until his regrets take the place of his dreams.

If you have doubt about doing something, ask yourself if you would do it if it were the last hour of your life.

Our golden age is never the present age.

After all is said and done, no matter how famous or important a man may be, the size of his funeral is going to depend a lot on the weather.

It matters not how a man dies, but how he lives.

If you think we have it bad, consider the average life span of a major league baseball is seven pitches.

Life does not cease to be funny when people die any more than it ceases to be serious when people laugh.

The bitterest tears shed over graves are for words left unsaid and deeds left undone.

They say such nice things about people at their funerals that it makes me sad to realize I'm going to miss mine by just a few days.

When you were born, you cried and the world rejoiced. Live your life so that when you die, the world cries and you rejoice.

<blockquote>
There will be two dates on your tombstone
And all your friends will read 'em,
But all that matters is
the little dash between 'em.
</blockquote>

Index

Break the rules, forgive quickly, kiss slowly, love deeply, laugh uncontrollably, and never regret anything that made you smile.